LOON CRY

SELECTED & NEW MICHIGAN POEMS

ALSO BY FLEDA BROWN

POETRY
Reunion (University of Wisconsin Press, 2007)
The Women Who Loved Elvis All Their Lives (Carnegie Mellon University Press, 2004)
Breathing In, Breathing Out (Anhinga Press, 2002)
*The Devil's Child** (Carnegie Mellon University Press, 1999)
*The Earliest House * (Kutztown University, 1994)
*Do Not Peel the Birches** (Purdue University Press, 1993)
*Fishing With Blood** (Purdue University Press, 1988)

ESSAY COLLECTION
Driving With Dvořák (University of Nebraska Press, 2010)

CO-EDITED VOLUMES
On the Mason-Dixon Line: An Anthology of Contemporary Delaware Writers (with Billie Travalini) (University of Delaware Press, 2007)
*Critical Essays on D. H. Lawrence** (With Dennis Jackson) (G.K. Hall, 1988)

*as Fleda Brown Jackson

FLEDA BROWN

LOON CRY

SELECTED & NEW MICHIGAN POEMS

THE WATERSHED CENTER   GRAND TRAVERSE BAY   2010

COVER AND INTERIOR ART BY GLENN WOLFF.

BOOK DESIGN BY HEATHER SHAW.

MANUFACTURED IN THE UNITED STATES OF AMERICA

CONTENTS

PREFACE

In 1918, my grandparents were invited by a colleague of my
grandfather at the University of Missouri to visit them at the
cottage they'd just bought in northern Michigan. It's on a lovely,
clear little lake, they said, with sandy beaches for the children.
The cottage they'd bought had been an old TB sanatorium
and there was a little green "guest cottage" with a wrap-around
screened-in porch that hung over the lake so the patients could
"take the air." This is where my grandparents stayed. The cottage
is still there.

Near the end of that visit, my grandparents took a walk along
the shore and came across a small white cottage for sale, $800.
They closed the deal, long distance, over the winter. This was
the year my father was born. In the early years, the family took
the Pere Marquette train north in the summers, had their heavy
trunks sent ahead. They were met at the station by a horse and
buggy and taken to the cottage a mile down the lake. When they
needed groceries, they rowed to town. My grandfather read a
book on swimming and taught himself to swim, then taught the
rest of the family as well as many neighbors. For years, there was
an enclave of academicians on that side of the lake, all swimming
properly.

Many people have tried to describe what a summer cottage
means to a family over generations. I simply can't. Our lake—
which we always called Central Lake, after the town, and only later
learned that its official name (equally uninspired) is Intermediate
Lake—is my own lifeblood. I learned to walk along its shores, I

have been swimming in it every decent summer morning all my life. I want to spend eternity swimming breast stroke from our dock on down to the wider part of the lake on a slightly misty morning. The lake has saved my soul many times.

So, in gratefulness, I put this collection together, selecting from all the lake poems I've written over the years, and including some new ones. And since the water is so much a part of who I am, and since the Elk River Chain of Lakes, which includes Intermediate Lake, supplies over 60 percent of the surface water for Grand Traverse Bay, this book is my gift to the water. All proceeds from the sale of the book will go directly to the Watershed Center, whose mission is to protect Grand Traverse Bay and its entire 1,000-square-mile watershed. The steady and passionate advocacy of the Watershed Center makes a huge difference to this region and to all of the Great Lakes.

As I've always said, when I get so old I can't do anything else, I want to sit on the end of our dock and watch the sun go down. I want the water to be as beautiful and healthy as it was the day I was born.

—F.B.

LOON CRY

Hope
then to belong to your place by your own knowledge
of what it is that no other place is, and by
your caring for it as you care for no other place, this
place that you belong to though you do not own it,
for it was from the beginning and will be to the end.
                    —Wendell Berry, from *Sabbaths 2007*

Let us all be from somewhere.
Let us tell each other everything we can.
                    —Bob Hicock, from *A Primer*

NIGHT SWIMMING

DOCK

Say *dock, dock*: it's just a hollow
of itself, the way the foot
echoes between wood and water,
the plank, plank of it
like piano keys, growing hollower
farther out under the stars.
Listen to the way *dock's* closed in
by the tongue on one side, pushed out
at the far end toward the lake
with a duck-sound, quack-
sound, where they congregate
for crumbs. It's even a tongue,
itself, saying nothing but
what you bump against it.
Or an arm, reaching out. Here
you're willing to make yourself sociable,
declare yourself separate
from the trees. "Dock here,"
you offer. Here is a place
to stop. And it's true. Indeed,
I have to stop at the end,
and think. The reason
for walking out here is
how the end goes blunt.
You feel your blood turn back
toward the heart, but
for an instant, you imagine,
it longs to keep moving out
like Roadrunner at the edge of a cliff,
keeping on with nothing built
to hold him up. Turning back,
I carve a cul-de-sac in the air,
which is a comfort, and a sadness.

3

LOON CRIES

Unless there is a loon cry in a book, the poetry has gone out of it.
—Carl Sandburg

Three loons appear in this poem, two
on one side of the canoe, one
on the other, but

not stable. One drops down
to nothing, emerges two minutes later
twenty feet away, quavering

his black beak's cold cries
across us to the others like a natural
bridge: oo-AH-hoo. Three loon cries

arise in this poem
from a hollow carved out
of itself, the slosh of what it says

to itself, not to us.
We four in the canoe sit
in the open AH, riding low as loons.

No one knows who feels
what, or how much. The grieving
syllables lie over us, untouchable

oo-AH-hoo, yodeled
oo-AH-hoo. Oh Lord, if we knew
what we can take from each other, and what

we have to leave alone,
if we knew which maniacal dives
the universe was thinking of all along.

4

OUT BACK

Once I heard an owl
through a tunnel from the moon,
imagined it huge
in its eyes, floating down
from the woods toward the lake.

All things moved down,
the life of trees clawed
at the hill, roots rolled
downhill in rivulets
beneath the lantern.
Behind my back, the cottage
slid toward the water
like an ice cube melting.

"See the eyes of the owl,"
my grandmother said, holding
the lantern to the trees
where something stirred, but
even the eyes had closed
into the awful dark.

My grandmother stood lean
and erect, her hair already loose
for the night and waved down
her back like the real woman
in a fairy tale. She said
my name, which was also her
name, said it out at the night
to make me appear, and hold.

BLACKBERRIES

Richie Osborne and Tom Ross
discovered Dave Roberts
about a mile up in the woods
behind the lake
in a one-room red house
papered with magazine pictures
of movie stars and boxers.
They'd listen to his blow-by-blow
of the Joe Louis/Max Schmeling fight
and the last Louis/Marciano fight.
They said it was like
a ringside seat, Old Dave's hair
shaking in his words.
After someone moved his house down
close to the crossroads so he could
pick up his groceries, all of us
used to climb the hills
to the wild blackberries
and bring him a jarful of the hard
and bitter things, since he couldn't
go back that far himself anymore.

WHALER

I teach my niece Elizabeth
to let down her oars,
then pull and lift with mine.
Our wake smoothes
like a tail. Elizabeth says
we are a dragonfly,
double-oared. I think
we are an old woman,
our low whaler spreading
the reeds with wide hips,
sloshing hollow.
Elizabeth talks nonsense
about Indians from Moscow
who spray their hair
with Raid. She imagines
molecules, red against
green, jostling the lake
like Jello. Sure.
And there were wildcats once
across the road, eating
the Knowles's chickens
and eating the loser of
hide-and-seek, who
would be thrown to
the night by the boys.
Flashlight/night,
lofting and sinking, we make
these exultations of oars.
We're always close to flying.
We always plan to fly.

NIGHT SWIMMING

We are without our men, hers dead
ten years, mine far away, the water
glassy warm. My old aunt already stands
half in. All I see is the white half,
her small old breasts like bells,
almost nice as a girl's. Then we hardly
feel the water, a drag on the nipples,
a brush on the crotch, like making love
blind, only the knives of light
from the opposite shore, the shudders
of our swimming breaking it up.
We let the water get next to us
and into the quick of losses we don't
have to talk about. We swim out
to where the dock goes blank,
and we are stranded, abandoned good flesh
in a black of glimmering. We each fit
our skin exactly. After a while
we come out of the water slick as eels,
still swimming, straight-backed,
breasts out, up to the porch,
illuminate, sexy as hell, inspired.

STONES

Cousin Al remembers the old game
he's still good at. You take
a stone from shore, large enough
to pull you to the bottom, but not
so big you can't bring it back
to hold the bank in place.
You swim out until the bottom
is as far below as you can bear.
Al shows me how to clear
my ears as I drop, but as soon
as they feel the squeeze, I see
how hard the stone pulls
down, how slow my rise will be.
My mother will finally leave
my father holding the refrigerator
door open, still explaining
geography. Aunt Cleone will forget
even yogurt, fade into silvery
fur between the birch trees.
My daughter will finish
graduate school, my son become
a computer programmer. The sun
will rise and set on opposite sides
of where I was last seen. This
is one second before my hands
let go the rock. I am a woman
on the way up: lungs, stomach,
heart, uterus, all my precious
cavities holding their own.
No doubt Al's won again, already
pushed off from below. Me, I'm
composed of space and the fear
of space. They break
the surface arguing like lovers.

SUNDAY AT THE LAKE

We all arrive at the Congregational Church
where on this particular Sunday the "Messengers
of Melody" from Muskegon are singing
the sermon. Irvin, his vest wearing his name,
squeezes out "Jerusalem" as if he knows something
urgent we should do. Then the whole group sings
"Marching in the Blood-Washed Band," and then
the youngest boy tells how the kids on his bus
all play their rock 'n' roll, but he has to
let them know he likes God's music best. After
this we shake hands, and outside I pick
some malva along the curb for Aunt Cleone,
and we coast to the restaurant, my father
swearing durnit he's not going to use
gas downhill. We all order the chicken dinner special
except Aunt Cleone, who spreads out her wilting
malva on her purse in her lap, and eats it
a sprig at a time. She asks her share of the bill,
but we tell her the water is free. After that
we go home to the cottage, where my father gets out
his screwdriver and tries to adjust his Westclox,
which has lost three minutes overnight.

CROUCHING

The day as nudging, as a nudging-stick, bark-stripped
and made to rattle across the storm drain grate,
hit the horse apples down, scrape along the sidewalk
and come, suddenly, to the deep crack, trace the crack
to its end, and the next, as if the cracks were a river,
a little portaging. There was no reason, no reason
to have a reason, and there was the creek which ran
over rocks for no reason, and the day opened
and closed like an eye to the ebb and flow of us into
and out of yards. I give her the name Sharon,
the only name I remember from those early ones. Julie—
Dick, maybe—not in the adult way of connection
involving exchange of information, but of moving alongside of,
poking beetles to see if they move, the crouching.

Tragedy, then, more like a shadow, not
the dead baby robin in its half-embryonic whiteness,
not anything precise and possible to reach with the stick,
but huge and uncontrollable, parental. I want
to poke with the stick so that the hugeness will remain
in the upper atmosphere, not here where I am crouched.
What is the material at hand? The mink ate the baby ducks,
John Pixler killed the skunk and the raccoon. Light hangs
in the air after the rain. A man in Springboro, Ohio,
caught the record longnose gar weighing 14.72 pounds.
Did I mention that little glistenings have formed on the lake?
The terrible noises in the upper atmosphere are quieter
when I look into the microscope. There was all that
outside my bedroom door, and inside were the poems.

THE GARFISH

They gathered on the dock after dark,
children and adults, with flashlights—
not to catch the two gar,
because a gar's inedible—but because
of their horrible prehistoric snouts,
the slow turning of their underwater
swords, each a separate thought
sure of where it was going:
no, worse, each
a hard impulse, bearing down
from some planet unknown to
the wobbly moored rowboats,
the delicate beached canoes.

Then she and Noah went over
to the house and stabbed the bass
he'd caught before, stabbed it
twice with the dull kitchen knife
to stop its writhing, and noted
its gills still pumping, head
cut off. They were happy
with the blood, the guts, in the old
way. It was the old and ordinary
story, the silent movements,
a thousand years, and before that,
the firmament, which must have been
all the meaning there was, until
memory shone its light upon it.

ELVIS AT THE END OF HISTORY

It was him, Elvis, sheepishly
stepping out of my outhouse,
looking better than ever, the way
some old men slim down and loosen
their lines. He had left the door open,
the lid slightly ajar on the women's
hole. As usual, I forgave him
everything. I acted normal, as if
I hadn't been waiting under the trees,
last night's full chamber-pot
balanced in my hand. I could have
said at any point in my life
that he was the one I was waiting for,
looking sleepily down from the stage,
seeing but not seeing me,
granting me reprieve in an instant
from my life, but holding me in it
like a star. It's like if you ask
for Jesus, Jesus comes. It's never
the way you think. There he was,
hair flopped over his eyes,
coming out of the last outhouse left
along the lake, and it there
only because of the grandfather clause.
This was the end of our history
together, all that strangeness
in the crotch, the pulse hammering
the bass line, real life and art
straining to fuse, to end all
history. I was hearing in my mind
Won't you wear my ring,
around your neck? but it sounded

like the sweet core of good taste,
like the gospel fleshed out,
saddened down to honky tonk.
"Excuse me," he said. "The older I get,
the more often I have to pee."
I agreed. I might have been humming
to myself, sometimes I don't know
when I'm doing it. I can be
treble and bass at the same time.

MINNOW

LEARNING TO DANCE

When we waltzed with the senior citizens
at the Pappy Burnett Pavilion,
I felt how you moved slick as a cowboy,
my own rough bones clicking beside
you, trying to move the way trying can't
go. I loved you, turning in yourself
like a loose skin, and the woman
who danced with her broom, and the old man
round-dancing, his shirt open over
his heavy belly, an old, old grace
feeding him from the bass
of the country band. I've always
wanted to dance. Aspen leaves tambourine
in the wind, needles flare from the tamarack
branch like ballet skirts, and that
Wednesday of the Central Lake Pavilion Dance
travels miles in place, turning
and returning to its original dark.
Afterward, I pulled off my swimsuit in the lake
and held you next to me, learning
from your heart and the slap slap of waves
on stones. What is it wants us to know
where to step? Each pause
brings us tight against the mouth
of the earth, and then we raise one
foot like the flame of a candle.
Our bodies move in and out of the space
we've held to be true, and something else
sees each half turn as the whole dance.

THE LOCATION OF FLEDA PHILLIPS BROWN

I think my grandmother stays mostly
in this part of the lake, maybe
up to Birch Point,
down to Deepwater Point,
her ashes churning behind big boats,
rocking against the shore, ashes
in the perches' mouths,
ashes in the ribbon of sun
under the water, ashes raining
through the hemlocks.
Before I found out, I had one
definite story, me, on my knees
on her iron bed, running the ivory
brush down her hair while she
found the book's good distance
from her eyes, went on,
in her school-voice:

              "Rather than
study grammar," said Gigino,
" I would change myself into an ant,
one of those ants that go about
always on parade, and do nothing
but march from morning to night."
So heaven turned Gigino into
White Patch the Ant, who carried
his little spot of earth
like a briefcase, learned
what it means to work.

Waves of loosened braid,
yellow and iron down her back,
that close I came to touching her!
For thirty-five years,
after the funeral in East Chatham,
or Troy, where I heard they had
folding chairs and Beethoven's Ninth
on the phonograph, she
brushed against me on all sides,
a fine grain. All that
about work: she could have just
opened my pores and passed through,
and did, and nobody told me anything.

MINNOW

It is not the way it used to be.
Aunt Cleone is losing her memory,
my father refuses to paint the cottage porch,

the rowboat rots in the yard. I am
willing to let go of what I remember,
not completely, but let it open out

into the past and fill it and funnel
forward to this place where I actually
lie on the end of the dock swirling my finger

in the water, watching the minnows
move without seeming to move, invisible
twitches, one, two, three minnows the color

of sand. I must be in the middle
of my life, the way I feel balanced
between one thing and another. As if I have

no hands or arms, parting the world
as it reaches my face. Like a minnow, gone
on little wings, a blush of sand from the bottom.

Sometimes I open my eyes in the dark
and it feels as if I'm moving. I lose
my loneliness, surrounded with dark, like water.

FOR GRANDMOTHER BETH

Just one scandalous year past our
grandmother's death, the second wife
stood homely and trembling ankle-deep
in the lake, taking on water and family
at once. Once, she told me, your grandfather
found the box of hair your grandmother
saved when she had it bobbed. She said
he cried, and I tried to imagine both
wives working it out in heaven. He took
this second one, taught her theories of
economics, gave her his grown children
and grandchildren, money and houses. They
used to sit at the kitchen table and eat
prunes, the same table where he ate
prunes with my grandmother. Regularity
took him to ninety-five, although
the last year in the nursing home
he couldn't remember who she was, and even
years before that, at the lake, he'd
call her by his dead wife's name. No,
Harry, she'd say, it's Beth, Beth,
and lead him back to where he meant
to go. She never touched the money
he left her, saved it for his children,
took in roomers and lived on interest.
Now she's dead and all Garth Avenue
is gone from me, from us, the house,
the lilies on the valley on the north side,
oh, it would be a long list,
and who cares now but us. This
is what I have to say for her, who held

a place and saved everything as if
she had no needs or wishes, except
to be no trouble at all, and to die quickly,
a light turned out to save electric bills.

CATCHING TURTLES

The slightest drip of a paddle
is too much. Let the canoe slide
by itself into the rushes and lily pads.
Lean far over the bow, your arm
a dead stick, drifting its shadow
through the water.
                    You scoop
a turtle from behind, snatch it
from the log, a hard bulge
escaped inward.
                Snappers, you grab between
your careful fingers, arched
across the shell, back from
their craning dinosaur necks,
their mute bird beaks.
                When you miss, you hear
the soft blip. Bubbles trail off
in deep, iridescent angles.

You don't catch them
for any reason. They scratch around
the canoe's wet bottom, leaving
stinking pools, and you bring them
two miles home. For days they wallow
and scrape their brown helmets
in the aluminum tub by the dock.
You add mussel shells and a Petoskey stone
for company. You feed them worms,
grubs, and a granddaddy long-legs.
You get used to hearing them.

When you go to swim, or sit
at the end of the dock feeding
the clamoring swans at sunset,
you start believing that skidding
and shucking against the tub
            is their real voice.
But when you let them go,
they ease down the rocks and slide
unruffled and heavy as fishing lead
under the alien weeds
in righteous silence.

MY FATHER TAKES MY RETARDED BROTHER
SAILING

They tack up and down
all morning, Mark trailing one hand

in the waves, crying his hard
gull-cries of joy, my father pointing out

bright flags on shore, which are
us, waving

them on, until
the sudden commotion of sail, jabber

of cleats, swingabout of
boat, pivot of Central Lake on

my father's foot, caught at that moment
in a rope,

my father hanging neither up
nor down, thrashing under, using,
                        maybe using up his lungs
to catch that child who hardly knows
water from air. The thought,

oh yes, the thought settles
in my heart: part of me

goes down, drowned, the perfect part
splashes back

27

to shore. And then years
later, here I come,

bringing out the towels, willing
as a murderer, reformed, but sentenced

anyway, to this life, to this
abundant life in which they have both

come back, my father's ankle bloody
from the rope, my purple-lipped

brother riding his shoulders,
                          uncontrollably babbling.

CHICKEN BONE

I can almost see my mother
rolling her eyes, trying to
get her breath, my father
coming behind to do the Heimlich
maneuver in Mrs. Pete's restaurant,
Mrs. Pete herself — she of the
$4.95 dinner, dessert included —
stepping in to do it right.

Before this, what?
They are talking about the heat,
maybe, the grosbeak
on the feeder, the rusting screens.

How long could that go on?
The menu could take a while.
A missing earring.
This is the way they
spend their lives
in our absence, this and
The Young and the Restless.
        "I'm finding out what makes
the young restless,"
he says.
        We children and the soaps,
swarming around their chicken
and mashed potatoes
like starved ghosts,
while they behave politely
to each other, God knows —
charity and violence having closed
together above them like

a little tent at last: the third
thing they've refused to speak
of, the limit to everything.

Guess what they do now? They figure the tip
on a napkin, not one cent
extra for the life they're in.

AFTER THE RAIN

While we are having breakfast
on the screened-in porch, waffles
with blueberries, my mother wrinkles
into tears over nothing, some
remembrance. She is always
giving in. The outside world is
wrung out, too, exhausted
with last night's rain, darkened
and earthly. On the black tree trunk,
a nuthatch pitches itself
upside down and sideways,
pecking wildly for bugs
under the bark. A chickadee
is a quick breath, lifting
off a limb. I want
to take my mother's hands,
but they are almost transparent,
terrible on the table.
Her body hunkers like a vase,
accumulating sorrows. It is
a Chinese vase, slender
at the neck, glazed
on the inside. In my mouth
are scrambled eggs
I have to eat or never get up
again. I sit through adolescence,
adulthood, safely
into menopause. The eggs soften
in my mouth, harden on
my plate, yellow ruffles.
Blue flowered oilcloth clings
to the table. My mother's hands
keep on fluttering

outward. No use, no use.
I pass her a waffle, butter,
the jug of pure
maple syrup, too heavy to pour.
I line up these items
in front of her. Hope
tries to get out of my chest.
It sounds like my heart, but it's
furious, hungry, light as a bird.

AUNT CLEONE WORKS HARD AT RECYCLING

After dark, Aunt Cleone happens across
the trash bags stacked, and begins to go through them,
finding strips of perfectly good
cloth to wash, cans to flatten, bottles to soak
the labels off. She is sad for our waste,
and she gathers armloads to her room,
stacks flattened cardboard under her bed,
lines up bottles on her shelves.
All these! Where's the next breath
coming from? Her mother's and father's voices,
beloved and quite saved, grow smaller,
the way the two of them turned to dots, swimming off
in the morning sun toward Snowflake.
But then back again.
Her mother's black wool swimming suit
still hangs on its nail like a bat.

In the morning, she has forgotten
the trash. I find it in piles on the kitchen floor,
what she forgot when she fell asleep, sorting.
She sits on the porch, stitching
someone's old blouse to fit her.
"Look," she says, "at the sunlight
reflecting like fire on the white sides
of the sailboat. It burns, but it never burns
anything up."
That's what I see, looking up.
Looking down, I see tiny suns dashing
like stray curls off the bottom of the water.
I notice we've kept the same sun and moon
we've always had, among all the suns and moons.

SCAVENGERS

SCAVENGERS

They're out there rattling their trailers:
the pickers, the carrion birds,
bone cleaners, the shadowy
alley dogs, sniffing
out fish under the trash,
their sharp noses neither
moral nor immoral. Fiber
that moves through the arteries,
cleaning them out. I think
of Wilson, Lloyd George,
Clemenceau, after the Big War,
of the ducks dipping to the bottom
of the shallows, of the Romans after Greece.
Especially I think of the earthworms,
eating eighteen tons of debris
in a year; the ground full
of earthworms going at it,
extruding, making soil,
and of 100-foot-thick glaciers
scraping it off, and of the sun
carrying off the glaciers,
and of combustion carrying off
the sun, and of death having
no dominion because
of the yearning that is always vast
and mysterious, a secret assignment
of the blood to find what it needs
(my items I left by the side
of the road—a rustle, and the rocking chair
gone in a half hour,
the desk in an hour, wind
at the edge of a cliff, things

taken the way the breath
is taken), turning the body
back to before words
began to wound the silence.

CEDAR RIVER

The earth is laid down dead
and alive at once, soft
and leaking from every vein
into the utterly clear creek.
Under the cedars a dead deer's bones
gather against the shade, the teeth
in the jawbone still firm
and musical, surer than my feet
through here. A porcupine big
as a small bear climbs unafraid
among the logs. Her quills
are streaks of sunlight and shade.
She walks back into the woods
with a sleepy ease
like a pregnant woman. I try
to follow across the weave
of roots, but it is like being
underwater. She crawls
over a mound of washed-up
twigs, one heap of twigs
becoming the other, like a Picasso
painting, and all over
the trees, eyes watching
from their separate
branches, separate planes.
I try to sort them out, using
logarithms, exponents.
One Grass-of-Parnassus flower
stands at the edge of the bracken
almost in the water, five white
petals with five purple
veins, hard little rivers headed
straight for the center of the world.

TRILLIUM

Named for its trinity of leaves, of petals.

The universe prefers
        odd numbers. It leans,
                obsessed with
what's next. It likes syllogisms,
        the arguments of
                sonnets: if A
equals B, then C.
        The ground-level
                common denominator,
the blood-red whorl
        at the base, is not
                an answer but
a turning. Does that leave you
        dizzy?   What can I
                say that would
reassure either of us? Even
        our prayers have to
                catch hold
as if we grabbed a spoke of
        a merry-go-round and tried
                to convince
the universe of what we want
        stopped, reversed.
                What it gives us
instead: this bad-smelling
        beautiful bloom.
                "Let go, let go,"
is what it says, and who wants
        to hear that?

SMALL BOYS FISHING UNDER THE BRIDGE

1
I watch them try and try for nothing
but tiny bluegill, sunfish, crawdads even,
anything to feel a tug, though they'd call it
necessity, as if they had to feed a dozen mouths.
They bend over the night-crawlers
with a whopping knife, too jagged, in love
with tools, machines, reels.
They're serious, removed, all of them,
threading half-worms as bravely as they can,
leaving me out of it, trying to act as if
the oozing is normal, required, after all
they've been taught about kindness.

2
It's excitement and mystery under here,
a boat churning through, echoing against
the bridge, and Zach, pulling up his bluegill
at last, shining and flapping.
He stops its fins down with his fist.
The fish looks at him, one eye at a time,
from its other world. From this one, the meaning
seems clear: the yanked hook, the yellow
plastic live-well barely wide enough for a fish.
But there's the human to figure in,
the complications of its mind, as it crouches
beside in splashed and sticky shorts.

3
After the hammer-blow, it's not so hard
to scrape scales into a universe of stars,
to saw off the head, fish-quivers
giving way to plain flesh.

What lesson can be learned by this?
It seems like no lesson
on the blue-willow plate—only eating
or being eaten, which turns out at last to be
a quiet exchange, nothing that could have been
helped, desire being what it is,
and fish like little knives
pointed toward it all the time.

—for Josh, Zach, Noah, and Daniel

LIGHT

I don't want to get started on such a nice night, but when I'm
standing out here and the security light's blasting from the boathouse
over the way, incessantly headed my direction
as light does across water and I can't see the stars only orange
bug-light and the nasty-wasp jet-skis angled half out of the water
and who's going to roar off on them at night anyway and I'm
without the big dipper or the little or the entire dark past
or the crawdads under the dark, and even swimming nude
is problematical in that glow that's intended to mean I try to figure
what, *here we are in the suburbs, maybe, because the dark's
dangerous,* and me, I like to walk out barely seeing my feet,
just flicking on a light at the end of the dock, not to go
too far, and then when it's off I'm floating with only the upper
world breaking through in pin-pricks we've given names to,
in our idleness or fear, but nothing like this tactless yowling
of light. Wouldn't you think there'd be boundaries, like when
a car drives by rocking with bass and I can't hear
myself think, wouldn't you think there'd be some respect for
people's secrets, invisible as they are, some acknowledgment
that the invisible's worth something, that I'm here, that there's a god
of some sort that picks up steam in the dark spaces, the more
dark, the more chance—so I try to turn my back to the light,
but is it awful of me now to remember Krackow, Kabul,
Monrovia, the yellow bombs in the night saying *Kilroy Was Here,*
to want to stand on this dock representative of my version
of history, declaring no more light, no more sight of jet-skis
taking no risks with their noses in the air, wouldn't you think
the dark would finally get angry, at least in my lifetime,
and I could watch the retribution, the darkening, that the stars
would begin to reach earth with their clear messages, that they
would have something to say after all that distance about traveling
through their opposite, doesn't it seem reasonable that I would
want to stand on the dock and wait for them to arrive?

JACK IN THE PULPIT

The Jack in the Pulpit folds
            over itself like a safety pin.
                  It's deep
in the woods, the hatchling
            of a dream in which
                  the red-veined
and phallic manages
            to seduce you with
                  the graceful curve
of vestments. You might
            like to think of it
                  as a small ship
with sail unfurling
            toward a New World,
                  the excitement
of discovery—yours—but
            it acts more like
                  a held tongue,
because when you can't go
            anywhere, privacy
                  becomes your grace.
What did Donne know,
            or Jonathan Edwards?
                  The air itself curls,
and down inside, only
            a hummingbird is able
                  to figure it out.

ODE TO THE BUFFMAN BROTHERS

Timmy so big he's awkward as a loon on land,
       but when he gets on his backhoe
           and his brother Luke on his Bobcat,
you can believe we were born for machinery.
       They get the big maple ready to go,
           Timmy rubs the backhoe's neck
against its trunk, slowly up and down until
       it begins to crack, as we all would,
           and falls through a perfect tunnel
of trees, wild hair every which way, Luke
       scooping it, and the smaller ones,
           into the huge dump truck. Then
they really begin, Timmy with his delicate
       biting and scooping, clanging the small head
           down on the cement walk,
lifting a chunk to the dump truck
       like a dead mouse, Luke backing
           and twirling in place. They do-se-do
to the low rumble of motors. They come right
       to the edge of the cottage foundation,
           they bite out a row
of stones around the old ice-house, they leave
       a perfect cliff, you should see it,
           roots exposed like the wiring
of the world, the smell of dirt and rocks and roots.
       Another thing: yesterday, they said,
           at six-thirty a double rainbow
landed about here. They said it was a once-
       in-a-decade rainbow, and I missed it.
           This is what I mean about them,
what I can't get enough of. They make me
       want to start over from scratch.

FLYING ANTS

They appear like spots in the eye, no explanation,
    dozens of them, winged, huge, on cue as the sun
        hits the eating porch between five and six, down
the wall, not attacking exactly, but clearly bound
    for permanence, checking out the territory. Swatting
        and spraying notwithstanding, they bring
their friends, feeling their way down the door,
    a prophesy. So okay, I call the exterminator;
        I toss my Buddhist prohibitions as if I've never
sat on a cushion. I sincerely dislike their clever
    hinged bodies, their fierce faces you can barely see
        under their flailing antennae and broad banshee
foreheads coming on like the final chapter, and what
    can one do—that's the point—against their gut-
        instinct mindless as a lynch mob? I can be
having my glass of wine, evening sun striking
    the lake at its low sparkle-angle, but my mind
        keeps turning corners, alert for signs
of trouble, working hard to slow the pace of things,
    preoccupied as Jesus watching in the garden for wings,
        only the welcome kind. Sometimes it's so
lonely on this earth, so much I don't know.
    Even the sky has its other side, and soon will let through
        only glints of what now seems true.

FOR MY DAUGHTER'S FORTIETH BIRTHDAY

Particles that were once connected will, when separated,
behave as if still connected, regardless of the distance
between them. —John Stewart Bell

Einstein called it "spooky action at a distance."
I'm rubbing my nose, and what are you doing,
now, dear one? What parts are we putting together?

I dragged you into this. What age is like, really,
I had no idea: turns out, the present settles
into its nest of memories and likes it there, even

when it stings. Let me start over. I am walking
North Intermediate Lake Road on October 7th,
not long till your birthday, sun on spider webs—

stop-signs of dew and sun, one after the other,
strung across stalks, a bloom-field of sun-charges
with their studious lines to the center. Time's

turned out to be my subject. It climbed
the ladder of my attention, spinning its internal
juices, never using itself up. It hasn't been pushy.

It's begun to feel like my best friend. Let me
start over. Memory's not as easy as I said: it muscles
horribly upwards, sometimes, bigger than I am,

carrying nasty details in its arms. I keep eating them
like a spider, so not everything will come your way.
I like to think of you where you are right now,

driving kids to school in Massachusetts.
I'm walking the lake road in Michigan, watching
leaves turn and burn in the eye of Time.

How dear it is to me, the way it holds you in its sun-
dazzled arms as you round a curve and brake
at the sign, squinting your dozen little wrinkles.

NO HERON

Herons are bigger than egrets, though they have the same long legs.
My father said one with an eight-foot wingspan flew over his boat.
I would like to be shadowed by something that big. It would seem

like poetry, just out of reach, moving and making a bare flush
of wings, and I would think of it long after, the way it was heading
away from me. My longing would not be satisfied even if I could

grab its scrawny legs in my hand, even if it nuzzled up to me.
I would be looking up the origin of *heron* with my free hand, and
when I read Greek, *to creak*, and Old High German, *to scream*,

I would wait for it to begin, but it would not say anything to me
in this boat which I am not in, but at my desk hoping for the heron,
a big one, as I said, so I can say, "Wow, look at that!" as if I were

getting up a circus. Out there are herons white and blue, not really
blue but smoky, with wings bigger than their bodies, dipping and
standing motionless beside lakes and rivers. Out there are universes

expanding until the space between atoms is too far to do anyone
any good. Thus, somewhere this minute one heron is calculating
the distance between his beak and a fish, the way it shifts. It is

as if he travels in space until heron and fish are swallowed into
each other. There is no heron at my desk. In fact, the absence
of heron is how I would define my study: no heron on the ceiling,

no heron on the floor, no heron on the wall, so that of course
I think of nothing but heron, how it floats its weight on one leg,
for example, flying that way even when it's not.

49

DAISIES

These flowers left by the mowers, white petals
wheeling around their yellow eyes, breeze-bent:
it's easy to switch on the sentiment, but no matter

which petal I land on, he may love me or love me
not. The daisy never did have any interest in my
childhood, either, my touching efforts to cheer, my

fistful of stems ripped up by the roots. Likewise,
it's empty of any responsibility to decorate summer.
Empty, too, of the mists of morning and the soft

thud of deer hooves in evening. It has no need of
rhyme or any other holy thing. It does not reject
its own death; indeed, it would be lost without it.

Sin, too, and redemption: rain and sun—why use
fancy words? Why exercise enthusiasm? To be alive
doesn't require enthusiasm, simply an adherence

to format, a multiplication and differentiation of cells.
So, I'm walking along, picking daisies, thinking
of Whitman and Dickinson, even Swinburne, thinking

how futile to keep on with my words day after day,
with the family clamoring for attention, declaring
that only I can fill the void in their lives. Or is it me,

thinking I'm the one, the answer to everybody's prayer,
the one with the recipe for Elegant Chicken Casserole?
Still, I make a large bouquet, bring it home, shake off

the ants, put it in a teapot. It says "I love you,"
in a Hallmark kind of way that at least is understood
by most, a gesture in a field of hopeful gestures.

LETTER HOME

THE KIND OF DAY

Sun on the water's bouncing ripples
      to the top of the big pine

as if the world's underwater!
      The air's so exact

on my skin there's no air
      and no skin, the kind of day

that's not a kind of day but
      a peeling back, the kind

of day I keep restlessly trying
      to use well because it's so

absent of difficulty. It requires
      taking on the thought of mist,

of rain, it requires making trouble.
      I don't know how peace

can stand it. I pick wild mint
      and chew it up, I pick

purple aster, Queen Anne's lace,
      even they are leaning

toward nothing, fields already golden,
      the word *golden* humped up

at the front, tumbling at the end,
      so easily it feels

motionless, the sky itself only
        an exhalation of the earth

into so many capillaries it can
        no longer be identified

as itself. The kind of day that
        makes you give up hope,

out of sheer frustration,
        which of course is just when

the centaurs and the acrobats
        finally have a chance.

LETTER HOME

Grass River is a snake on the tongue.
You, love, a thousand miles down
the map, many turns. Meanwhile,
I am plunging ahead here through
forget-me-nots, marsh marigolds,
Joe Pye weed, and underneath,
the bright fur of mosses,
moss over moss, tangled, unspoken,
this great green marsh bleeding
everywhere.

               Speckled trout line up
like knives under the falls; strings
of moss weave and pull, one
hard pull, everything part-
ing, everything in slits, peaks
of reflected light, teeth, laughter.
If you were here, it would be
just the same, only two,
taking on whole the foreign language
of the birds. It would cling
to nothing in us, and we would still
be hungry together, teeth, tongues.

HAWSERS

Things *must* return
from their journey outward—
the frayed ends of hawsers,
bones whitened and lightened,
feathers (bedraggled
is the only word for it, like a dog's tail
through mud) —
must return from the dolors
to their primary colors.
Humans have a stake in such
things—the eye's eye
with its three cone receptors,
the mind's eye that ties
everything up in three dimensions.
Sometimes, though, a small,
fish-shaped, slipping
curve, comes

RIBS AND CANVAS

The old canoe was ribs and canvas and whispered
like a duck's trail. The new one looks almost
the same but is made of poly-composite that won't
wear out and won't break through if it's dragged
across the rocks. People aren't as careful
as they used to be, she thinks. Few care to paddle
slowly down the sunset listening to ducks
and watching the first bats jitter overhead.
They're all inside with their TVs. So many
reasons to be sad. Beyond the Rosses' dock,
just deep enough, there's been for years a heap
of tires and two old boats, to draw the fish.
She sees these when the water's still. Her paddle's
been repaired with string and glue. It's held
this way for years; it makes her feel less lonely
among changing things: the different water
of the lake, the pine tree's different cones,
the Knowles's house no longer Knowles's. Her ideas
of America, icons emptied long ago,
if they were ever full. She's all gut-feeling,
in the canoe, perfectly happy to be there,
well, not perfectly, well, not happy, but content,
well, if she knew what happy meant, she might
choose that. There's only words. She's stuck with them
now: they come up like turtles, float on top
like lily pads. She imagines on her deathbed
giving up this constant strain to see
beneath the shimmer. She'll pull the covers to
her ears. Someone will bring mums dyed
those awful colors, and someone else will bring
Khalil Gibran, and, like you-know-who, she'll walk
across and never once look down.

WILD TURKEYS

1

Wild turkeys, necks jutted out, wattles flapping,
heads and bodies turning, all the same creature,
coming from somewhere, going back to somewhere,
ragged black and blood-red as if they were half-dead
already, chewed up. They remind me of Poe's bird:
ghastly, grim, and ancient, ugly as Roy Orbison,
or George Eliot, ugly as Sir Robert Walpole, Lyle Lovett,
Eleanor Roosevelt, the ones who radiate ugly until
a person begins to lust after it. Lust like street kids,
pants below their underwear, hair screaming
bloody murder, shoving beauty out of the way,
as if the sonnets, the great waterfalls with their tropical
pools, even Brittany Spears, were all distractions
from the fierce entropy, the smashed and flying glass,
like bits of bodies blown from tanks.

2

The motion at the edge
of the woods is the turkeys with horny splay-feet
step-gripping with their sure knowledge
that the earth is what's moving, not them.
They're holding on with the purposefulness of the damaged,
the infirm, the wretched, who've put all their interest
into survival until they're lean, coded, all meaning
the same thing. I get this way, the old pain gone
but still on the edges, a damage of the heart
that doesn't hurt now, but knows what it feels like,
the turkey-head, the beak: the real things that went on,
the divorces, or rather, the agonizing over them,
my mother's death, or rather, the agonizing over her life.
It's the surroundings and not the thing, the ugly things
I've made out of my thinking, what I've hung onto,
my deep sleep of hanging on, while the wild turkeys
go on back and forth across the road, oblivious.

DEER

It was the deer. Or the raccoon lumbering away
from the feeder. It was America, pretending to be
innocent. I wanted to show you the deer because
we like to point out the wildness on our land,
as if the animals chose us from among contenders
for our purity of soul. The red foxes especially, the shier
the better, to show how far we are from McDonalds,
from Hummers. I wanted you to count the deer
with me, to agree that we love the world, the one
that can't be bought.

                Some days the sun disguises things.
What's missing out there burns in our eyes.
We rant about politics. We feel like survivors
from a dangerous life. We enter books, looking not
for foxes but for accurate punctuation, a good phrase.
We want to be part of something lovely. We love
the idea of deer—remember when there were twelve
roaming along the creek-bank in the snow? Maybe not
in snow. The snow stands for the page, how far
they have to travel to get here, how we can't
turn them away no matter what our hearts
are like, because of their alertness. We need them
for an alarm, for the terrible unnatural strangers.
The kids smoking outside the mall on a school day
are like those deer. They have muscles they might use
at any minute. They're perfectly made for escape.

                Meanwhile, we live with these windows,
this deck, and the wandering of animals.
We watch TV. It's ridiculous the way we sit here,
the way we talk, as if possibilities for relieving the poor,
stopping the war, were public, waiting, longing
to be enacted. Tails go up like flags. Under the tails,
the fierce smell, a dignity. Who knows what to do,
when everything keeps so far from us?

PURE ROMANTICISM

I'm sitting on the ground, dampishly cool, glad
for sun after a long, dark winter, wondering if Beauty's

my own idea, or if sun is intrinsically better, less sad,
or agreed-upon-better, than clouds. If music—

the careful math of frequencies—is more sublime
than the noise of a 747 overhead. If I put

in a loon, now, or take my yellow kayak to the foot
of the lake and just sit there, my modest little chime

of waves not scaring the loon, if I put in the skree-skreee
of gulls, along with the mating ducks, and the lone goose

that desperately flaps to launch its wet freight
when I get too close—is this Beauty, or Truth,

or both? Not to implicate one thing (like nature)
in Beauty, but wondering if the mind is a necessary gate

to its entrance. If this were true, how would
happiness fit in? What if it's an ordinary day, pure

in the sense that it hadn't a thought, and no one stood
at the brink and thought for it? What if I were just

sitting here, bored, maybe, without any lust
for explanations? I can imagine Beauty's prodding me,

desperate for a recollection in tranquility, or just
any old acknowledgment of the daffodils nodding.

THE ROUTE WE TAKE

IF I WERE A SWAN

I would ride high
above my own white
weight. I would ride
through the lightening
of the earth
and the darkening,
stillness and turbulence
coming on in the core
of me, and spreading
to the hard rain,
to the dazzle. Leaves
would turn, but I
would keep my eyes
in my head, watching
for grasses. This
is what I would know
deeply: the feathering
of my bones
against the bank.
For the rest,
I would be the easiest
wave, loving just enough
for nature's sake.
The world would move
under me and I would
always be exactly
where I am, dragonflies
angling around my head.
Under the black mask
of my face, I would think
swan, swan,
which would be nothing

but a riding, a hunger,
a ruffle more pointed
than wind and waves,
and a hot-orange
beak like an arrow.

NORTHERN PIKE

Just past the railroad bridge
over the Green River, the deep pool—
dragonflies and white moths—
where you can see the huge
fish hovering. And Zach
with his skinny arms, leaning,
and the whack of the line,
the wrenching. I wish I could
save him from his nightmares,
his waking fear of muggings,
of bombs, of what there is
legitimately to be afraid of.
Up came the pike, nearly three
feet long, teeth set on the line.
I didn't see this. Zach came back
with the fact of it in his face,
terror and the joy of terror,
the pike down there in his soul,
making up its mind without
thinking, moving up and down
like a submarine by shifting
molecules of gas from its blood
to its swim bladder, not a motion
of the body involved, waiting
to clamp fish, frogs, children,
sideways in its teeth, nothing
to do with consciousness,
with will, and here is Zach
to tell me, as if I hadn't been there
myself, watching the worst
come up because I fished it
up out of its waiting, and almost

went down with it, to the green
and gloom, to the churning
ghosts. As if I hadn't won, too,
when the line snapped,
the weight of it lasting forever
in my skinny arms.

DO NOT PEEL THE BIRCHES

In his time,
germs were found to be everywhere,
especially in his ball-and-socket joint
which was welded together by tuberculosis germs
before pasteurized milk became a rule.
Grandfather ordered his shirts done at home
because (he demonstrated) the downtown launderer
spat germs on the iron to test the heat.
Flies (he caught mid-flight in his cupped hand)
could crop-dust germs over lunch,
and one's mouth grew germs quickly enough
between the meal and the toothbrush.

He gathered us at Central Lake every summer
to learn the rules. He explained the use of
lie (to recline) and *lay* (to place or put):
because of his lame leg, he could *lie*
comfortably only in the canoe, so we must
lay it gently on the sand, keeping its
irreplaceable wooden frame from rocks.

At Central Lake, one could get hold
of things that go wrong. One could nail a sign
on the birches to save their delicate skins.
One could avoid shampoos or detergents that foam
the lake. One could rinse diapers in a bucket
far up the hill to filter the dirty water
through the ground. One could wait
one full hour after meals, and only swim
across the lake guarded by the rowboat.
One could follow the rules and get results.
When Grandfather was ninety-four
he was still getting results.

In the cottage, he heard the wind chimes
answer to an ancient wind.
Someone pulled diapason
on the pump organ, and he called back
a perfectly metered hymn.
Muttering through the fir trees, he
was able at last to discuss the day's mail
with his dead wife, who knew what to do.
And every morning and evening,
he stoppered his ears, hitched his lame leg
over the dock, and buried himself in the lake,
only his nose rising for air. He broke through
the elements as cleanly as a machine.

CHICORY

I worry about the chicory, that tinge of pink
in the blue, its sunset delicacy, even with its tough
stalk. Those ragged, blunt petal-tips.
Like my high school Pep Club skirt, pleats
sharp as knives, but someone could easily get
under it. The road here is crooked, cars fly by
at 45 or 50. I worry about how few walkers
there are, how alone nature is, out there
sprouting and budding and dying. Can the utterly
unnoticed survive? What about the farthest
reaches of the universe, the other solar systems?
There's a lot that doesn't seem to need us,
but the negative space around the flower
is what shapes the flower, so the neglect
of such a powerful mind as ours must collapse
its bloom at least a little. So much reciprocity
necessary to exist: we actually exchange DNA
with those we catch diseases from. The germs
travel to our lymph nodes, carrying a bit
of our infector: we become our enemies!
The quality of our existence is that delicate,
which is why I ran from room to room, comforting
my mother, stacking up my father's mess,
wiping my poor brother's drool. No, that's not
right. I was only holding them all in my mind
to keep them from flying apart. How tired I was,
my little body a strung bow. How small
I'd keep things, little flowers by the roadside,
if I could. I would think of them day and night

WILD LILY OF THE VALLEY

Among the ordinary lilies
          of the valley, their bells
                    lined up neat
as choristers, you're the country
          cousin, tiniest sparkler
                    of bloom, stamen
projecting, nothing shy about
          you. And who isn't sexy
                    under the trees
by the lake, who isn't
          a little aggressive,
                    full of the need
to ignore the rules, to say
          something directly
                    out of the thunder
of ground, the whole dark
          that spawned us?
                    Nothing greater
than sex. The dark would run on
          forever without it.
                    You show up
with your frowsy equipment
          powered by two clapping
                    leaves, to unbalance
the civil town. Or, it may be
          my mind taking hold,
                    tangling desire
in my hair until it is all a Medusa's
          coil, something we
                    come to together.

YELLOW TROUT LILY, ALSO CALLED
ADDER'S TONGUE

Trout lily because its leaves look like
        little trout, all mottled;
                Adder's tongue because its

sharp-tongued petals turn perversely
        backwards. What flower
                hasn't been gilded with

language, or photographed into
        an elegy of nature? Furthermore,
                how shall I ever

give up High Def, now that I've got it,
        the way it makes the world
                brighter than

the world? I flip from channel to channel
        in a trance that feels like
                married love,

nothing left out: Rush Limbaugh
        on Larry King, PBS special on
                Saving the Chesapeake,

Mayberry R.F.D., the President on Oprah.
        The wild lily meanwhile just
                opens its delicate

mouth all the way down to the hollow
        of its sex, barely a passage
                made out of itself.

MONARCHS

The monarchs blink
along the buddelia bush, eye-level, acting like
the butterflies of my childhood, except
for the one that fights its way
to the top of the poplar tree.
All of them, though, are starting to agitate

over their upcoming trip to Venezuela —
who would have thought it? — little torqued-up
leather-wings, miniature thrusts,
as if someone had dropped
a Picasso and made monarchs, splintered
into Monet or Manet,

thousands of jewels —
diamonds — because a butterfly's wings
have no pigment at all,
only prisms that try to deflect attention
from the fiercely secret source.
Easy to imagine that one thing stands for another:

monarchs erupting
wet from a former life, baptized by immersion.
Forgive me, I only recently learned
they have no former life. The caterpillar melts
down to pure DNA. It is not a matter of reshaping,
as if it had a sex-change operation. It is

a monarch, finally
shed of whatever sluggish thoughts
had dramatically misunderstood what life this is.

RED PAINT

Here is my father, lying sideways on the dock
trying to scrub off blood-red marine paint.
Here are his old hands and forearms, bloody,
everything he touches, bloody. My words
are so bloody, as usual, I try not to say them.
I could be ten years old, mopping up
my brother's blood after another seizure.
My father's acting like he's ten, as usual,
smearing paint everywhere. If you knew
the history. I drive to the lumberyard
after paint thinner. "Don't move," I say.
I douse the dock with thinner, too.
"Oh for heaven's sake," he says.
"In World War II, they used to splash red paint
on the decks to get the men used to blood."

        "Oh well," I say, because he will die
sooner than later, because the sun is a white eye,
and I've cleaned up the dock under the willow,
because the water's sloshing, gone and permanent
in its way. Because his sailboat's sleek with red,
a missile cradled on sawhorses.

        "Merely cosmetic," my father says
about my cleaning, as if I've wasted
my life. *A body doesn't like to spill,* I think.
*Not even light spills. Look at the sun, stopped
by leaves, trunks of trees. There are sorrows
like hot stones, they give birth in silence.*

There is my Mother scrubbing a bathroom
in heaven, folding sheets, getting to have

her version of nice. "Mother," I say, to remind
the universe I'm here, holding back with my
bare hands what still needs holding back.

PHOTO OF HER FATHER

At that moment, gorgeously 18 or 20,
headed down a wooded path,
legs of his overalls flapping, shit-grin,
shirtsleeves rolled like a workman's, pen
in pocket. Has he been lonely since?

Is he satisfied? The daisies along the path,
the slight blur of trees overhead, make her ache:
that moment, charged with before and after,
the father who is not yet a father (assuming

there's a stable self, assuming that everything
starts someplace: say, the word *Father*).
She wants to pin down a beginning, a trajectory,
a "once" that gives birth to an end. No matter
if it comes down to *Father forgive them.*

There's her father, his bent old body,
pinioned by itself, constipated,
heart aided by stent. The path, if there was
a path, got made by the making. What
was cleared, or cleared away?

Is he stepping through? Who can she turn to,
who could be the everything and nothing
that made her? That moment of pure delight?

THE ROUTE WE TAKE

Six Mile Lake

The lake is a droop of space
and we are paddling in it,
remote and yearning.
An old man and woman start out
in their pontoon boat that sputters
weeds. We find them again,
farther on, fishing. The woman
has balanced her hips on a twig
of a chair. The man spits
at the water as if he has arrived
at exactly the right place.

Ellsworth Lake

A root floats up,
a gladiator's arm,
brown-studded, crooked.
Cut, it feels like cork,
or something you could
eat if you had to,
one thing standing for
another, and nothing
as horrible as it looks,
snaked underwater.

Green River

We follow the mink along
the bank until it climbs
into the tangle of roots
where water has risen
and fallen. We see through
to clearings, stammers
of light, a few sharp red
cardinal flowers, a whole
network of traces, not ours.

Wilson Lake

Two great blue heron jut
fantastically, pterodactyl-
beaked, carrying the sky
to a cold distance. The high
sun sinks its teeth
in the waves. We arch
our necks after the bird.
The last thing we want,
we tell ourselves, is
intelligence, or comfort.

Benway Lake

Uncle Dick says they subpoenaed
the farmer who penned hogs
across a feeder-stream,
their raw fecal matter
launching out, greening.
We stop and wade to where
the cold appears invisible.
We actually drink from our
hands, praying for innocence.

Hanley Lake

A row of old docks slope
and dislodge like disproved
theories. We observe
the sequence
of them, heavy and frail.
Lily pads collect
at their feet to soften
the failure. The day
is full of sunshine. We have
our canoe, our traveling.

Central Lake

Late evening, we pass
through the needle's eye
of the bridge. Our big
voices briefly catch
between the concrete roof
and black water, before
we open into our own
wide lake, our faces
extinguishing, no one to tell
if the paddle is feathered,
no crucial place.

THE DEATH OF CLEONE

            Of course she mistook
her son for her husband, since
it was the lake, and summer,
and she had grown small and turning,
as if the world were a kaleidoscope and she
its center made only of mirrors.
It was his voice, his hair, his height, so she
let down her own white hair and set her lips
on his before he realized. Still, when he
held her hand at the end, he was willing to be
anyone, and he talked to her of Central Lake
again, and when he reached the edge
of words, he took her arms
and made a motion of paddling
the canoe, and she did open her eyes
across the small craft of her bed, gliding
out into the last sliver of sun.
She passed the dam at Bellaire, through
Clam River, Grand Traverse Bay,
Lake Michigan, into the dream-soup
of details, of J-strokes. It was hard work
against the drag of water, before she
remembered she was a gull, and the water
turned to air. No, not a gull. Not that far
to go. Only back to Central Lake; she was
one of the ducks lifting off, pulling up
their landing gear in their awkward
duck-flurry of voices, and it didn't matter
which one she was, or who it was that
loved her, all of them winging around
within the hollow of the lake.
So began the silence, the evening,
the turning stars.

ACKNOWLEDGMENTS

Most of the poems herein have been selected from previous
collections of poetry by the author with the generous permission
of the editors of the following presses:

From *Fishing With Blood* (Lafayette, IN: Purdue University Press,
1988), "For Grandmother Beth," "Out Back," "Blackberries,"
"Whaler," "Catching Turtles."

From *Do Not Peel the Birches* (Lafayette, IN: Purdue University
Press, 1993), "Do Not Peel the Birches," "Minnow," "Learning
to Dance," "The Route We Take," "The Location of Fleda Phil-
lips Brown," "Loon Cries," "Night Swimming," "Aunt Cleone
Works Hard at Recycling,""Stones," "My Father Takes My Retarded
Brother Sailing," "Sunday at the Lake," "After the Rain," "Cedar
River," "Letter Home," "Dock," "Elvis at the End of History."
From *Breathing In, Breathing Out* (Tallahassee, FL: Anhinga Press
2002), "Monarchs," "Chicken Bone."

From *Reunion* (Madison: The University of Wisconsin Press,
2007), "The Death of Cleone," "Trillium," "Small Boys Fishing
Under the Bridge," "Light," "Red Paint," "Ode to the Buffman
Brothers," "Flying Ants," "For My Daughter's Fortieth Birthday,"
"No Heron," "Jack in the Pulpit," "Wild Lily of the Valley."

Poems in these collections first appeared in the following publications:

From *Fishing With Blood*: "Catching Turtles," *Mid-American Review.*

From *Do Not Peel the Birches*: "Do Not Peel the Birches," Indiana Review; "Minnow," Sycamore Review; "Learning to Dance," "If I Were a Swan," *The Iowa Review*; "The Location of Fleda Phillips Brown," *The Beloit Poetry Journal*; "Cedar River," *Mid-American Review*, "The Route We Take," *Brigham Young University Studies*; "Night Swimming," *West Branch*; "Dock," *Stone Country.*

From *Breathing In, Breathing Out*: "Monarchs," *Poetry*; "Chicken Bone," *Prairie Schooner.*

From *Reunion*: "The Death of Cleone," Poet Lore; "Trillium," *Southern Poetry Review*; "Light," "Small Boys Fishing Under the Bridge," *Arts & Letters*; "Red Paint," *Midwest Quarterly*; "Ode to the Buffman Brothers," *Image*; "Flying Ants," *Tampa Review*; "No Heron," *The Kenyon Review*; "Jack in the Pulpit," *Poetry.*

Grateful acknowledgment is also made to the editors of the following publications in which these newer poems have appeared:

"Chicory," "Northern Pike," *The Iowa Review*; "Daisies," *Ocho*; "Scavengers," *The Southern Review*."Hawsers" is part of a set of poems and sculptures in collaboration with sculptor Bill Allen and exhibited at the Dennos Museum in Traverse City, MI. "Photo of Her Father" appears in prose form in my collection of memoir essays, *Driving With Dvorák* (Lincoln: University of Nebraska Press).

Publication of this book would not have been possible without the generosity of Heather Shaw, who donated her time and skill to design it and to oversee its production.

GLENN WOLFF grew up in Traverse City, Michigan. He studied Printmaking at Northwestern Michigan College, and received his BFA from the Minneapolis College of Art and Design in 1975. Moving to New York City in 1979, he established a career as a freelance illustrator and over the next decade his clients included the *New York Times*, Simon and Schuster, Alfred Knopf, *The Village Voice*, *Sports Illustrated*, *Sports Afield*, *Audubon*, the Central Park Conservancy, and the New York Zoological Society. In 1987 he returned to Northern Michigan illustrating numerous books including the critically acclaimed *It's Raining Frogs and Fishes* by Jerry Dennis, and *Flight of the Reindeer* by Robert Sullivan. He now concentrates on fine art and his work has been exhibited in galleries and museums across the U.S. and Canada.